JUJITSU
BASIC TECHNIQUES OF
THE GENTLE ART

JUJITSU
BASIC TECHNIQUES OF
THE GENTLE ART

by
George Kirby

Editor: Gregory Lee
Graphic Design: Karen Massad

Art Production: Mary Schepis

Twenty-eighth printing 2006

© 1983 Ohara Publications, Inc.
All rights reserved
Printed in the United States of America
Library of Congress Catalog Card Number: 83-60127

ISBN-10: 0-89750-088-1
ISBN-13: 978-0-89750-088-3

WARNING

BLACK BELT BOOKS
A Division of **OHARA** 🔲 **PUBLICATIONS, INC.**
World Leader in Martial Arts Publications

ABOUT THE AUTHOR

George Kirby has been a serious student, teacher and proponent of jujit-su since his introduction to the art in the early 1960s. Kirby was awarded a shodan in 1968 from Sanzo Seki. In 1969, Kirby and his associate, Bill Fromm, formed the AJA. Kirby currently serves as the AJA's president and chairman of its board of directors.

A native of Los Angeles, Kirby earned his bachelor of arts and master of arts degrees in Social Science at California State University, Los Angeles, in 1969. He acquired a state teaching credential and is now a junior high school instructor with the Los Angeles City Schools.

Kirby has actively taught jujitsu and basic self-defense classes from 1968-75 at the Burbank YMCA and since 1974 for both the Burbank Parks and Recreation Department and the Los Angeles City Schools. He was awarded the 1981 AAU Jujitsu National Sports Award, a certificate of honor from the Federation of Practicing Ju-Jutsuans, and was voted Outstanding Instructor in both 1971 and 1974 by the California Branch Ju-jitsu Federation. He was promoted to godan in 1980.

Kirby has written numerous articles for *Black Belt* magazine, and has authored three editions of *Budoshin Ju-Jitsu,* a comprehensive compilation of jujitsu techniques used as a workbook in many jujitsu classes. He is also an active organizer and judge at tournament competitions.

An avid backpacker and photographer, Kirby prefers working in and around his San Fernando Valley home with his wife, Adel.

INTRODUCTION

Jujitsu is the "gentle art" of self-defense. It is an ancient art that has received, unfortunately, little notice in the 20th century. This is due to a number of related factors. There are few instructors that are qualified to teach jujitsu in the United States as compared to the other more popular martial arts of judo, karate, and aikido. Most jujitsu instructors also teach through local YMCAs or parks as they choose to teach for the enjoyment (as their sensei did) rather than at a private dojo where finances and livelihood can become a concern.

There have also been very few definitive writings on the art in contrast with the other martial arts. This book will attempt to shed some light on the art of jujitsu by defining the art, presenting its history and philosophy, and giving instructional guidelines that will help the serious student develop his knowledge. This book will also present a number of techniques that will start the student on his way toward perfecting the art as a means of effective self-defense. Upon satisfactorily perfecting the techniques presented in this book a student will be somewhere between a purple belt (fourth kyu) and a third brown belt (third kyu), according to the standards of the American Ju-Jitsu Association, an internationally recognized governing body of jujitsu in the United States. AJA tests have been included at the back of this book for handy reference.

This book could not have been possible without the time given by two jujitsu professors in training me over the years. I'd like to take this opportunity to express my sincere gratitude to Jack Sanzo Seki, hachidan, jujitsu, for taking me under his wing in the 1960s and providing me with the opportunity to learn and teach the art under his careful guidance. Gratitude must also be extended to Harold T. Brosious, rokudan, Ketsugo jujitsu, who showed me another facet of the art. Without these two giving people this book would not be possible. Additional thanks must also be given to my wife Adel, who was patient with me during the process of writing this book, Kevin Harte, nidan, and Robert Harte, shodan, who gave their time to help shoot the pictures, and the staff of Ohara Publications who worked very closely with me to perfect this book for your education and enlightenment.

—George Kirby
Burbank, CA
January, 1983

Jujitsu: The Gentle Art

History of Jujitsu

Jujitsu has not had a neat, organized history as many other martial arts have. It is easier to trace a martial art when there is a single source from which it began. It is more difficult to trace the roots that form the base of an art. Such has been the case with jujitsu.

The practice of jujitsu can be traced back in history more than 2,500 years. Jujitsu (*ju* means gentle; *jitsu* means art) developed from many individual teachings that either originated in Japan or found their way to Japan from other Asian countries. In 2674 B.C. the first mention of martial arts comes from Huang-Di (China) who founded *wu-su* (martial arts), a concept in which the body was used for self-defense purposes. Going far back into Japanese legend one might be able to trace jujitsu back to the ancient Japanese gods Kajima and Kadori who allegedly used the art to chastise the lawless inhabitants of an eastern province.

The first dated mention of jujitsu was during the period 772-481 B.C. when open-hand techniques were used during the Choon Chu era of China. In A.D. 525 Boddhidharma, a Zen Buddhist monk, traveled from India to China, visiting the Shaolin monastery. He soon combined Chinese *kempo* (*kenpo* in Japanese) with Yoga breathing to form Shaolin chuan fa (shorinji kenpo in Japanese[1]). As legend has it, Boddhidharma eventually developed the system further into what became *go-shin-jutsu-karate* (self-defense art of open hand). In 230 B.C. the wrestling sport of *chikura kurabe* developed in Japan and was integrated into jujitsu training. Approximately 2,000 years ago there is also mention of the development of wrestling and related techniques that served as the base of jujitsu.

---

1 Shorinji is the Japanese spelling of the Chinese Shaolin. The Shaolin monastery is considered to be the source of sil lum kung fu.

There is evidence that empty-hand techniques were in use during the Heian period (A.D. 794-1185) in Japan, but in conjunction with weapons training for samurai. In A.D. 880 Prince Teijun (also known as Sadagami) formed the Daito-ryu Aiki Ju-Jitsu school. Daito-ryu aiki jujitsu was based upon the secret teachings of *shugendo* (*shu* means search, *ken* means power, *do* means way), the eventual source of kendo which used circular hand motions to assist in defending oneself with weapons. It was from this school that Morihei Uyeshiba took portions of the art to start his own system of aikido in 1925.

Most of the actual credit for founding the formal art of jujitsu goes to Hisamori Tenenuchi who formed the school of jujitsu in Japan in 1532. In 1559 Chin Gen Pinh, a monk, migrated from China to Japan, bringing kempo with him, parts of which were integrated into the current teachings of jujitsu. During the Tokugawa era (circa. 1650), jujitsu continued to flourish as a part of samurai training.

The next historical phase of jujitsu, which had gone into decline with the closing of the Tokugawa era, was in 1882, when Jigoro Kano developed the sport of judo from jujitsu in order to increase the popularity of the martial arts and to provide a safe sport using selected techniques taken from the art of jujitsu.

Jujitsu in the West

Jujitsu made its way into the United States in the early 20th century. Although there are historical accounts that indicate President Theodore Roosevelt practiced jujitsu, it actually may have been judo. A significant influx of the art was first felt in Hawaii and on the Pacific Coast of the United States in the period between 1920-1940, during which time a number of Japanese migrated from Japan. A second influx was felt following World War II when a number of United States military men returned from tours of duty in Japan.

There is no single style of jujitsu in the United States today. This is perhaps a weakness. Jujitsu has been called many things in the United States, from one form of karate to a synonym for judo. This may be a consequence of the Americans' desire for simplification, or ignorance of what jujitsu really is and where it came from.

Regardless of the style of jujitsu, practitioners all seem to cover the same ground even though there may be different emphases, and elements may be taught in different sequences. The art has survived, though, and that is its strength. It has been flexible enough to endure through the ages and grow, once again, in today's world.

Jujitsu Defined

Stated simply jujitsu[2] is the *gentle art* of self-defense. This is a very simple definition for a very complicated art. It does have a more complex definition. If we look at the many characteristics of the art it will be possible to come up with a more complete definition, one that is more suitable for the serious student.

First, jujitsu is what might be called a *parent art*. A parent art is an art from which other martial arts develop. Since jujitsu has such a broad history it was inevitable that other arts, or more correctly, *ways* would evolve from it. Ju*do* (gentle *way*) and aiki*do* (the *way* of mind and spirit) can trace direct lines to jujitsu. Many styles of karate, especially kenpo, can also trace some of their techniques back to jujitsu. Therefore, in addition to being a parent art, jujitsu is also a combination of many of the more popular martial arts taught today. Upon observing a practitioner of jujitsu one will see flashes of each separate *do*. One will also see how many separate moves can be combined into an effective self-defense system.

Jujitsu is a series or combination of techniques that have been separated into other arts. Why was jujitsu separated into specific *do* or ways? Jujitsu may have become too complex as an art or, because there was no single system or systemized way of teaching it, too difficult to learn. Both Kano and Uyeshiba were able to simplify and systemize their ways. There are perhaps 30 to 50 basic moves in jujitsu. However, it is the combinations and variations of the basic moves that make the art so complex and almost infinite in its variety of moves. By dividing the art into three general areas (judo for throws and leverage, karate for strikes and hits, and aikido for nerves and the use of attacker momentum), portions of the art would be easier to teach. They would also be easier to organize and perpetuate as a system.

As they become easier (a relative term) to teach, organize, and perpetuate as a system, the *way* would also become more attractive to potential students. I am not placing a value judgment on the validity of *any* martial art, as all arts are effective when placed in their proper context. I am merely presenting one logical possibility in the evolution of the martial arts. Jujitsu was in decline in 19th-century Japan, a time period when other martial arts were on the rise. Jujitsu was a complex art. The other martial arts were also complex, but because they could be organized and limited in their scope they became easier to teach. Their growth was inevitable.

---

2 Jujitsu can also be spelled *jiujitsu, jujutsu,* and any number of various ways, but they all refer to the same art.

Jujitsu ultimately survived by traveling two parallel pathways. There were those who continued to teach the art as an art, realizing that students would recognize the virtue of studying jujitsu and pass that knowledge on. There were also those who studied one of the *do* that evolved from jujitsu, became proficient, realized something was missing, and developed proficiency in each of the other *do* that make up a major portion of jujitsu. In their own way, they put the pieces of the puzzle back together again. It may not have been quite the same puzzle that jujitsu started out as, but all the pieces still fit. They were able to integrate judo, karate, and aikido back into the martial art of jujitsu to provide an effective system.

This theory of two paths can be borne out by observing the variety of *styles* of jujitsu that exist in the United States and throughout the world today. Despite their differences in terminology (and sequence in which techniques are taught) they are all remarkably similar. Many, in fact, are identical by the time the student gets to the level of shodan. It was my own instructor's belief that there are *no* styles of jujitsu—only the art of jujitsu.

Jujitsu is an extremely effective self-defense system. If jujitsu is taught as an art the student will have a vast resource to draw upon to defend himself with. He has learned a series of basic moves that can be combined in an almost unlimited manner. His only limitation is his knowledge and understanding of the moves and how and why they work. A skilled student can create and control the amount of pain his assailant may feel without any injury taking place. He can also create sufficient pain and disabling injuries that will make it impossible for the assailant to continue his attack.

If you give a man a fish he has enough food for a day. If you teach him how to fish he has enough food for a lifetime[3]. The same saying applies to the martial arts. If a student learns specific defenses for specific attacks he may survive *those* attacks. If he learns a variety of moves as an art he will not only survive the attacks but also develop a greater variety of responses to any given situation. He has been given the tools of survival rather than a simple meal.

If jujitsu is taught as an art a proficient student can use his knowledge to create new and different combinations of moves based upon the basic moves he has learned. That is how this book is organized. The student is encouraged to take the basic moves and combinations in this book, master them, and then reorganize them into other combinations. It will be like lighting the first candle in a tunnel. You'll be surprised how far you can go.

---

3 Anonymous saying.

Surprisingly, jujitsu is also a form of relaxation. There is nothing more rejuvenating than letting your developed *ki* (energy) control your situation on the mat. You don't know what attacks are coming at you and you don't have time to think about them anyway. It's a pleasure to let your ki control your own body, executing techniques smoothly, without your sensing any mental or physical output taking place. This is a skill that is acquired after much practice and patience. This is also what makes jujitsu an art.

A Philosophy of Jujitsu

If a person seriously studies any martial art it is inevitable that such a study will include the development of a philosophical background. It is also inevitable that, as a person grows further into the art, the interrelationship between the physical and mental aspects of the art will also be developed and strengthened. The result can be a philosophy of life in which the martial arts training serves as a base.

Such is the case with jujitsu. There is a philosophy that goes with the knowledge; there is a close interrelationship between the physical and mental aspects of the art; the resultant philosophy can have a profound influence on one's daily life.

There are a number of factors that affect a student's philosophical growth in jujitsu. The first factor is the destructive potential of jujitsu techniques from a purely physical viewpoint. A skilled jujitsuka can control his attacker's *ki*, which is the inner spirit, driving force, or center of energy. If a person commits himself to a course of action he is committing his ki; his ki is directed toward that end. The skilled jujitsuka can control that energy. As a student becomes more knowledgeable in the use of nerves and pressure points he will also develop the ability to create and control pain without doing any real harm to his assailant. Combine both of these elements with the ability to create real pain and disabling injuries and you can recognize the potential control and havoc that a skilled student can deliver to an attacker.

Because of this destructive potential, jujitsu places a strong emphasis on the concept on non-violence. A physical confrontation should be avoided whenever possible. There are two additional reasons that support this concept of non-violence. First, as the jujitsu student is confident of his skill he recognizes that he has a better than average chance of defending himself successfully. Thus it is unnecessary to prove he can if such a confrontation can be avoided. Second, a physical confrontation indicates that all rational means of resolving the problem have failed. It is humanly degrading to become involved in a physical confrontation—it indicates that reason and intelligence have failed.

A second factor that will affect philosophical growth is the knowledge that can be obtained by studying the art. In addition to learning the forms and moves of the art there is also the continuous process of combining and varying the forms to deal with the same or different situations in different ways. It is an infinite mental process. Once the student masters basic techniques and the ability to integrate them the result is greater confidence.

The ability to control one's *own* ki and an attacker's ki is a third element affecting growth. To control one's own ki the student must be relaxed. Learned techniques should flow from the center of the body automatically, spontaneously. The student can sense and use his attacker's ki only if he (the student) is relaxed. If the student can control his own ki it is possible for him to remain calm and in control of himself in stressful situations.

Fourth, an understanding of the *circle theory* can be of profound importance. At this point the circle theory will be stated simply: everything moves in a circular motion. For every action there is an appropriate consequence suitable to the action. This theory, with respect to the physical aspect of the art, will be dealt with later in far greater detail.

The last major factor affecting the philosophical growth of the student is the circumstances under which the art is learned. If the student is taught jujitsu solely as a means of self-defense, then that is all that the student will learn. If the student learns jujitsu as an art—perhaps for relaxation, as I did—he can gain much more. He can look at the art as an art form rather than solely as a means of self-defense. He can see *why* techniques are done as they are and what makes them work. Rather than just learning techniques he can learn to *understand* them. If he can understand them he can adapt them to different situations and integrate basic moves with one another, knowing in advance what the consequences will be. The process can be related directly to daily life.

The philosophy of jujitsu as an art is based on the concept of continuity. Within the teachings of jujitsu there is the concept of the continuous flow of things; by extending one's own ki one can control the ki of others and by controlling the other person's ki it is possible to control that person. As techniques must be modified to meet different situations so must we be able to change to meet new situations successfully.

Learning the art also involves developing a great deal of patience. Techniques are not learned and then put aside. They are constantly reviewed, improved upon, modified, and perfected. A good instructor will strive to train his students psychologically as well as physically, as my teacher did with me. "Words are cheap," Seki Sensei would always say. The higher in rank we became the more verbal harassment we had to put up with. The harassment served to encourage those of us who stuck it out to do better. It also taught us not to let words affect us, who we were, or our goals. To persist in our studies was our goal. Patience was the key.

By understanding jujitsu—the *art* and its concepts—it is possible to recognize that you can have greater control of your environment while accepting it at the same time. By studying the *art* you can develop a better understanding of the limits of your environment, yourself, and others. This is particularly true if you become an instructor. Students will come to you as clay, each one with a different malleability. You can do a great deal with your students if you nurture, mold, push, and recognize them. You can help them recognize their own potential.

With time and training a student will develop a feeling of self-confidence combined with humbleness; it is not necessary to always prove oneself. He can be patient, tolerant, and understanding of others—a real asset to growth. He will also develop greater self-control, recognizing that he can control his environment through confidence and an understanding of his abilities. All of this can give the serious student a positive outlook on life. Jujitsu can be learned as an art in all of its facets. It can give the student an understanding of what life is and how to be an active participant in it.

CONTENTS

Technical Principles of Jujitsu

In order to develop jujitsu as an effective means of self-defense there are a number of skills that must be acquired and developed. These can be placed into two general areas: ki development and the actual mechanics of techniques. If you practice techniques and moves regularly, your proficiency will be developed and improved. It is essential that you take your time while learning. Rushing will get you nowhere fast. Patience and persistent practice, directed toward perfecting techniques, will bring you the confidence that accompanies success.

Ki Development

Ki development is one of the two most important factors in making jujitsu techniques effective for self-defense. It is one thing to go through the mechanical moves of each form. It is quite another to execute them without any apparent mental or physical effort. Ki development will help make that possible.

What is ki? It is considered to be the *source* of power or energy in the human body, the cause of momentum when the human body directs itself toward a goal. Metaphysical tradition holds that one's ki is located approximately one to two inches below the navel at the hypogastrium or *saiki tanden* (lower stomach). That is where the center of our energy or center of gravity is located. It is the focal point for many jujitsu techniques.

Ki is also energy directed *from* the body. This concept is especially true in aikido and the many *te waza* (hand techniques) of jujitsu. In using these techniques the student directs his ki through his body and out through his fingertips in order to execute what appear to be effortless defenses against an attacker while not actually grabbing the attacker's arm or hand to execute one of many responses (a release, hold, takedown, throw, or come-along).

This is a difficult concept to explain. As my instructor explained it to his students, ki is like an electrical field. In order to use ki effectively it is necessary that the hand and fingers be relatively straight and relaxed so that they can direct the energy in the direction the fingers are pointed. If the fingers are bent with the fingertips facing your palm, or your fist is tightly clenched, it is impossible to extend ki, as it is redirected back into your body.

The same concept can be applied to all jujitsu techniques. You should always look in the direction you are going—never at your attacker—while executing a technique. If techniques are executed properly there will always be a flow of ki in the direction you are looking, or where your fingers are directed.

Ki development requires that you be relaxed, mentally and physically. Only under these conditions will your mind and body be at ease and receptive to your ki. You must be in a relaxed state to operate most efficiently. By being relaxed you can also sense and use your attacker's ki to your advantage. With a calm, clear mind and relaxed body you can more readily react (or anticipate) unforeseen changes and be able to direct your body correspondingly with very little or even no apparent conscious thought taking place. Admittedly this is not the easiest thing to do in a street situation but it can be done if the student is proficient in his knowledge and practices *on a regular basis*.

Ki development also requires that you learn how to use your attacker's strength which is concentrated in *his* ki. When attacking, your opponent will use muscle (that is, strength) to accomplish his goals. In the process he will create momentum and a direction of force. Recognizing that the attacker's strength will usually be greater than yours it is essential that you use *his* strength, not yours. If you are calm and relaxed it will be easier for you to accept and use his ki, *helping* him to reach his goal. In other words, you will redirect his ki or enhance it with your own to bring your attacker down in the direction he was directing his ki. It is possible and often necessary to use your ki to maintain control of the attacker and the situation.

Excitement, nervous anticipation and tenseness are your worst enemies. Any of them can cause your body to release large quantities of adrenalin, a hormone that enhances body strength during times of great stress. If you can remain relaxed you can control the adrenalin flow. If you cannot control its flow you may lose control of your body and your ki.

Jujitsu techniques will only work if you are calm and in control of your body. Calmness is reflected in your ability to keep presence of mind in an otherwise tense situation—even though you are well aware of what is happening or has happened and are scared. If you remain calm, keep your presence of mind, speak in a low voice and refrain from indications of fright, you have a better chance of surviving the situation successfully.

Smoothness in the execution of techniques will come with time, practice and experience. Jujitsu techniques operate best when done smoothly—one motion flowing into another—without any choppiness. Choppy executions will provide the attacker with the chance to regain control of his ki when your ki is not flowing smoothly. You will be successful when you can execute techniques without any apparent effort.

The key is not trying at all. Sometimes the harder we try to do something the more difficult the task becomes and the more elusive the goal. If you are relaxed and calm you have a greater chance of success. If you are relaxed your ki will do your work for you.

Speed cannot compensate for a lack of development in the aforementioned factors. Speed is a consequence that will come naturally as proficiency in techniques increases. Proficiency *and* speed are required for effective self-defense techniques. However, speed cannot compensate for a lack in proficiency.

It is also necessary to control the techniques you use for controlling the potential damage that can result to your attacker. Most states have laws that frown on the use of excessive force. While not being an attorney, I feel that it can be safely stated that no one will deny you the right to defend yourself. It is what you do in the process of defending yourself that may cause problems. Effective self-defense does not mean beating your opponent to a pulp. Self-control means doing only what is necessary to protect yourself.

Another essential aspect to the development of ki is your *kiai* (literally, spirit meeting), more commonly referred to as a loud, aggressive yell. There are numerous reasons for developing a good kiai. Practically, a kiai draws attention to your situation. Secondly, it should scare your attacker. Lastly, a good kiai makes it possible for you to completely extend your ki to control the attacker's ki when the situation warrants.

One last element in the development of ki must be explained. That element is flexibility. You and your techniques must be able to change as the situation changes. A person grabbing you may not warrant the same response as someone who is trying to hit you. Yet the first may be a prelude to the second. Anticipation can be a friend or foe. If we anticipate what is going to happen it is possible to plan for it. However, anticipation may also tunnel our preparations toward only one attack or direction. Flexibility can avert this negative consequence of anticipation.

Flexibility also allows one to smoothly move from one technique into another. Such flexibility is acquired after techniques are learned well and the mechanics of their operation are understood. It is this area that will be dealt with next.

Ki development covers many areas: relaxation, strength, calmness and smoothness, speed, control, kiai, and flexibility. All are interrelated and dependent upon one another. Ki development is essential for the proper execution of techniques. In jujitsu, ki is the key to success.

Mechanics of Techniques[1]

Jujitsu techniques are relatively easy to learn if you approach them with an open and positive mind. If you also understand the mechanics behind the techniques they are easier to understand and learn. For this reason some time will be spent here covering some of the general mechanics of the art before moving onto specific techniques.

All of the techniques in this book are taught right-handed. This makes it much easier for the vast majority of people to learn initially. If you are left-handed (as I am), be patient and learn the techniques right-handed. It will be no more difficult for you than a right-handed person. Once you've learned everything right-handed the student should then learn the techniques left-handed by simply doing everything opposite. At this point a left-handed person will usually have a distinct advantage as he has superior coordination on his left side.

All of the techniques in this book also require that the defender start all moves from a left ready position (*tachi waza*). This will allow you to start from a balanced position. Most of the techniques in this book are interchangeable. A technique used for a lapel grab can also be used for a hit, club attack, choke, etc., with only slight modifications in the initial reaction to the attack.

The use of strikes and nerves form an integral part of jujitsu techniques, either to loosen up an opponent as part of an actual technique, or as a finish to a technique once the opponent is on the ground. Nerves and pressure points are those points in the human body, usually at a body joint, where nerve centers can be attacked. The attack may be a simple application of pressure by one finger. This may result in controlled pain (with no injury), loss of blood circulation, or a stunning feeling identical to an electric shock resulting in a muscle spasm, numbness or muscle contraction, which can be used to loosen up an attacker. The use of simple pressure also makes it possible to control and redirect the attacker's ki.

A nerve or pressure point attack can also be in the form of a hit or a kick. In this case the amount of force is not as important as the speed at impact and how fast the hit or kick can be withdrawn. The strike is supposed to stun, not injure. Almost all hits of this type are done with the open hand. There are many successful stunning blows that can be dealt with the palm of the hand in a cupped position. Again, the intent is to stun, not injure.

---

1 Much of this material is quoted directly from my article, "The Artful Transition from Empty-Hand to Weapons" (BLACK BELT, December 1981).

The ability of the jujitsu practitioner to develop the use of nerves to create pain is based upon his ability to become proficient in the use of empty-hand techniques combined with an understanding of ki and the *circle theory* of movement. By acquiring a good understanding of empty-hand techniques the student will also have acquired an understanding of ki and the circle theory.

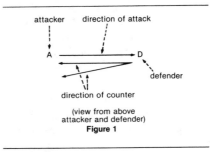

(view from above
attacker and defender)
Figure 1

When attacking, an attacker commits his ki to the direction of his attack. He is extending his center of energy in that direction.

When attacked you use your ki to stop his force and counter it directly as in Figure 1. Your ki can also be used to absorb the attacker's ki and either continue his direction of force or redirect his energy in another *complementary* direction as in Figure 2.

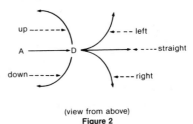

(view from above)
Figure 2

Attacker momentum is the end result of the attacker's extension of his ki. It is that amount of energy that is directed toward a certain point (Figure 3). The momentum, as an expression of his ki, is what is used by a jujitsuka as a basis for his response to the attack. It is the ability to sense and use the attacker's momentum that makes circle theory techniques possible.

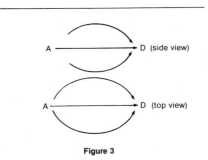

Figure 3

The circle theory is both a very simple and extremely complicated concept that deals with the movement of the attacker. The basic idea is this: through the use of the attacker's ki, momentum, nerves and pressure points, and the use of

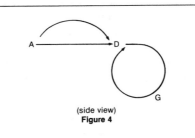

(side view)
Figure 4

your own ki, you are able to direct the attacker in any number of directions by extending his ki in a circular motion. To accomplish this the defender must become the center of the circle with his extremities serving as the spokes that radiate out to the edge of the circle. Figure 4 gives a basic idea of the circle theory. If an attacker (A) strikes at you with a hit or a club you move out of the direct line of the attack, deflect the hit, and then continue its direction in a circular motion, bringing the attacker down. The movement of the defender in directing the attacker's ki must *encourage* the circular motion. Even though the attacker may not make it beyond the ground (G) the motion and the ki must be extended beyond that point to guarantee success.

The circle theory also allows movement to the left or right (Figures 5 and 6); up to the right or left for a kick (Figure 7); or if against a knife thrust or swipe (Figure 8), a double circle—one to block the wrist and the other to execute the throw. The application and combination of circle theory movements are limited only by the defender's skill and knowledge of techniques as well as the attacker's ability to survive them (attackers rarely survive the defense).

You may have noticed that the moves illustrated in Figures 5-8 all involve changing the direction of

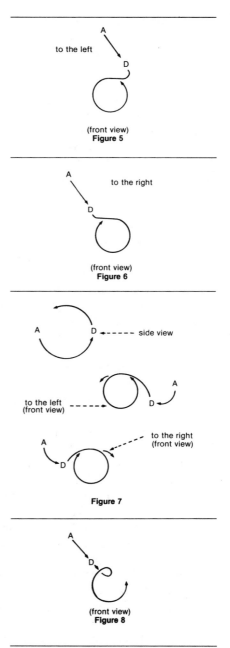

to the left

(front view)
Figure 5

to the right

(front view)
Figure 6

side view

to the left
(front view)

to the right
(front view)

Figure 7

(front view)
Figure 8

the attacker's momentum. This is accomplished by redirecting the attacker's ki in a complementary direction. A complementary direction is one that is *usually* less than 90 degrees to the right or left, up or down, from the direction of the attack. The change in direction is usually a circular motion incorporated into the circle that actually results in the throw (Figure 9).

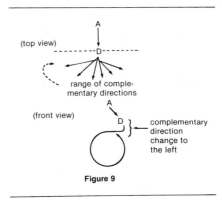

Figure 9

The chart on page 27 indicates sensitive points on the human body that can be attacked in a number of ways, either as a nerve attack or as a strike. If you choose to strike some of these areas for purposes of delivering a powerful blow it is best to use your elbow or kneecap. Both of these parts of the human body will allow you to deliver the greatest amount of force within a given area. You should be aware that any striking technique can cause severe injury, often internally, which can permanently damage your assailant, in addition to causing a great deal of pain and discomfort.

You and Your Partner in Practice

Learning jujitsu as an effective art and as a means of self-defense requires a great deal of practice. However, once learned it is extremely effective and very easy to do. Jujitsu techniques are only useful if they are automatic reactions. It is impossbile to learn jujitsu techniques without a partner. You must work with another human body to get the feel of techniques. All jujitsu techniques are taught as reactions to street attacks. There are no formal kata, as in karate.

The study of jujitsu requires two people who are willing to work together and trust one another. Basic to this willingness and trust is the requirement of caution and courtesy. If you are the attacker you must realize that your partner is learning techniques. Your attacks need not be overly aggressive. Align them with the proficiency of your partner. As you each become more proficient you can become more aggressive. In this way you can help each other increase your skill and self-confidence.

As the person executing jujitsu techniques you must be considerate of your attacker. Jujitsu techniques are designed to cause injury, usually breaking or dislocating an extremity at a joint. Linear fractures are a common result. (Linear fractures go up or down the length of a bone and are usually caused by excessive torque applied to the extremity.) Execute techniques slowly at first, gaining proficiency with each move. Executing techniques slowly will also allow your attacking partner to move in the direction you wish and thus reduce the chance of injury. As you become more proficient in your techniques, and your partner becomes more proficient in his ability to follow your techniques, you can increase your speed.

It is never wise to resist jujitsu techniques. Resistance can result in serious injury quite easily. Jujitsu is based upon ki and leverage, not strength. All your partner may have to do is exert an ounce or two more effort and you will end up with a sprain or fracture. There is a rule you can follow to protect yourself when you're being thrown: *go with the throw*. If you can't, or you're being submitted and the hold is set or starting to hurt, you should immediately indicate submission by calling *maitta* (I submit) or by tapping your partner or the mat until the hold is released. Don't try to see how much pain you can take or for how long you can take it. Subtle injury may take place that can have long-range cumulative consequences. Be cautious and courteous.

Proper clothing and a proper workout area are essential for safety. A single-weight judo gi is strongly recommended as the proper uniform. A judo gi will take the stress of jujitsu techniques without the risk of tearing. Because of this students can be more aggressive at learning as they don't have to worry about their opponent's clothing.

This has a very important street application. In a street situation you cannot worry about you or your attacker's clothing. Your concern is protecting your body. If you're worried about clothing you'll never be able to defend yourself. Using a judo gi helps dispel this concern. There is nothing more psychologically damaging to an attacker than finding himself thrown to the ground, possibly injured, and seeing his clothes in shreds. That's supposed to happen. You can create psychological fear in your opponent regardless of the amount of actual physical damage you have done to his body.

The second advantage of a judo gi is that it is fairly loose fitting. This will allow you to move more freely while practicing techniques. Admittedly one doesn't walk around the street wearing a judo gi. However, the intent is to learn techniques correctly and street clothes will hinder some moves or tear if you complete those moves. This doesn't mean that the technique is a poor one. It means that your clothes are preventing you from moving. What's important is that you're protecting your body.

Your workout area is equally important. A good minimum area is about

150 square feet of mat space. Do not use "exercise" mats as they don't provide adequate padding. Good mats are necessary for your own and your partner's protection, otherwise it is impossible to learn techniques effectively and without them it will be difficult to avoid serious injury.

You and your partner must assume a learning attitude on the mat. You must be willing to help each other learn the techniques correctly. This requires verbal and physical communication. As beginners you should cooperate with each other completely, learning how to do the techniques correctly. As you progress you can become more aggressive. However, please accept that when a hold is set correctly then you should go with the technique for your own protection. To do otherwise is to invite serious injury. On the other hand you shouldn't fall or go down for your partner just to make him happy. If you are truly friends, sincere in your desire to learn and help each other, you will help each other learn to do it right.

VITAL STRIKING AREAS

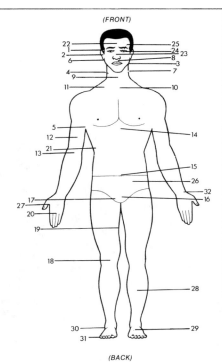

(FRONT)

(1) temples (left and right) (ms)
(2) ears (insert finger)
(3) under jawbone (ls)
(4) base of neck at artery
(5) under armpit, upward
(6) mastoid nerve under ear (ms)
(7) base of neck directly down from mastoid (lm)
(8) philtrum (base of nose) (ms)
(9) larynx (ms)
(10) below larynx at collar bone (ms)
(11) collar bone (ms)
(12) half-way between elbow and shoulder below bicep
(13) inside of elbow
(14) solar plexus (ms)
(15) hypogastrium (about 1-inch below navel) (ms)
(16) groin (ms)
(17) arterial pressure point (near)
(18) kneecap (ms)
(19) inside thigh
(20) hand (between fingers 3 and 4)
(21) right or left base of ribs (lm)
(22) center of forehead (m)
(23) nose (ms)
(24) base of eyes (ridge) (ms)
(25) eyes (s)
(26) bladder (ms)
(27) between thumb and first finger
(28) shin
(29) instep (ms)
(30) ankle (m)
(31) toes (lm)
(32) wrist
(33) base of skull (s)
(34) center of neck (ms)
(35) base of neck (ms)
(36) between shoulder blades (ms)
(37) kidneys (ms)
(38) back of elbows (m)
(39) heel (achilles tendon) (ms)
(40) back of knee
(41) rear crotch area (ms)
(42) rear side base of skull (ms)
(43) trapezius muscle

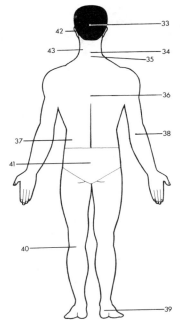

(BACK)

LEGEND:
(l) light damage (moderate or sharp pain)
(m) moderate damage (may numb or stun for short periods; possible injuries).
(s) serious damage (possible serious or permanent injury or fatality).

27

Preparations

Before we study the basic techniques illustrated in this text, it is necessary to cover a few basic principles and examples of falling properly. The importance of learning to fall cannot be overemphasized, as many martial artist of experience can tell you. Your dojo training will require you to take many falls, over and over again—especially in the art of jujitsu.

Knowing how to fall instinctively may be invaluable to you in an actual street confrontation if you are caught unaware and thrown off balance. You will be able to absorb the shock of a fall on concrete or other hard surface and avoid injury, enabling you to defend yourself further, or run away from danger.

READY POSITION

(A) The right ready position is a relaxed stance with your left hand ready to block (hand open and fingers together) and your right hand clenched in a fist ready to strike if necessary. The right foot is pointed about 45 degrees to the right of the direction you are facing. You should be able to look down and see the front half of both feet. The left ready position (B) is the exact opposite, with your right foot forward. Your body should not feel tensed.

BASIC SIDE FALL

(1) Start from a squatting position with your left foot out. (2) Let your body fall backward to the left side (don't jump) striking the mat with your left arm, palm down, as your hips contact the mat. (3) You should land on your left side with your legs apart and your head off the mat. Yell loudly (kiai) just before you hit the mat to force the air out of your lungs. (If you don't get the air out of your lungs before you hit, it will get knocked out. If you lose your breath you can't respond and get back up un-

1A

2A

til you are breathing again.) (1A) As you get more proficient you can work up to doing the side fall from a standing position. (2A) Be prepared to hit hard with your left arm and kiai to absorb the shock of hitting the ground. (3A) Your left arm should be angled about 45 degrees from your body for proper shock absorption. *Note:* You should practice all falls for both the left *and* right sides. Insert "right" into the above directions to execute falls on the right side.

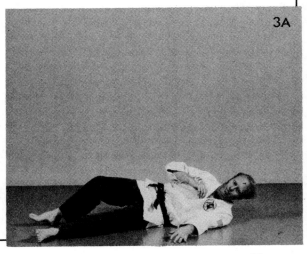

3A

BASIC BACK ROLL / FALL

(1) Start from a squatting position. Tuck your chin in. (2) Fall back, using both arms to break the fall. Both arms should slap the mat at about 45 degrees from your body. (3) Tucking your head to your left, roll over your right shoulder (4) onto your right knee (5) and then back up into a ready position. As you get more advanced you should try this from a standing position. Be sure to tuck your head in to your chest and break the fall with both arms. Do *not* reach back to break a back roll.

BASIC FORWARD ROLL

(1) Squat down, placing your right hand in front of your left hand. (Both hands should be turned inward slightly.) Tuck your head to your left and (2-4) push off with both feet, rolling up your right arm onto your right shoulder and then down diagonally across your back to your left but-

tock. (5) As your legs fall forward, break your fall (or forward momentum) with your left arm by slapping the mat. This will help absorb the shock and train your reflexes to slap the mat every time you are on the receiving end of a practice throw.

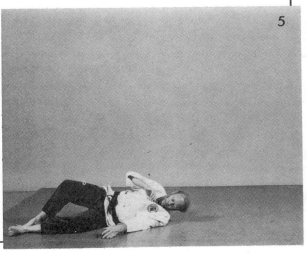

BASIC
FORWARD FALL

(1) As you get more proficient at the forward roll, work toward doing the fall from a standing position. (2) Make sure your hand is always palm down, whether or not it touches the ground. (Keeping it palm down lines up your arm and body muscles properly for a safer roll.) Remember to tuck your head in to your left. (3) Break your fall as your body is about to hit. (4) You should then tuck

your left knee under your right leg, (5) raise yourself up onto your left knee (6) and get back up in a ready position, turning at the same time to face your attacker. Avoid using your hands as you get more proficient because you will need your forearms to block any incoming kicks or hits while you are down. If you're using your hands to get up, they can't protect you.

Basic Techniques

Jujitsu, unlike arts that solely emphasize kata, is an art that must be learned through contact. Constant training with others is the only way to understand jujitsu and its usefulness. Keep in mind that some techniques will be more difficult to learn than others, and none can be mastered overnight.

The majority of the sequences that follow combine two techniques: first, there is a response (for instance, a block) to a specific attack, followed by a control technique or submission (such as a joint lock). The control techniques may be combined with different responses, and therein lies the almost infinite combinations found in jujitsu. Refer to the chart on page 120 and you will see the many different techniques that may be used to respond to specific attacks. Experiment with various combinations and you will discover how vast this art can be.

One book cannot possibly demonstrate all the techniques of jujitsu, but the sequences here will acquaint you with the most basic ones. This book is best used in conjuction with personal instruction.

BASIC ONE-ARM HIP THROW / WRISTLOCK-LIFT SUBMISSION

(1) Your attacker grabs your clothing with his right hand. (2) Grab his right sleeve with your left hand and (3) strike his solar plexus with your right fist as you move toward him. (4) Step to the inside of your attacker's right foot with your right foot. Your right arm goes under his right arm. (5) Pivot to your left on the ball of your right foot as you bring your left foot back. Both of your feet should be inside his feet (the heels of your feet should be closer together than the front of your feet, but they shouldn't touch). Squat straight down so that your waist is below his waist and his right thigh is resting between your buttocks. Hold your opponent tight against your back. (6) Lift your opponent off of the ground by straightening your legs and bending over at the waist. Let your leg muscles do the work, not your back. Throw attacker by turning to your left and looking to your left. Do not look at your attacker. Be sure your right hip is blocking his right hip. (7) Once your attacker is down, drop down onto your right knee and (8) bend his right arm down by slipping your left hand down to the back of his wrist and slipping your right arm under his arm, grabbing your left forearm. (9) Your left knee pushes down on the side of your opponent's head as you pull up on his wrist. If done quickly, the wrist will snap.

BASIC DROP THROW / WRIST-PRESS SUBMISSION

(1) Assume a ready position as your attacker is about to strike. (2) Block his punch away to your left with your left forearm, then (3) slide your left hand down to grab your attacker's sleeve, stepping across with your left foot. (4) Pivot counterclockwise (to your left) on the ball of your left foot as your right hand grabs your attacker's clothing on his right shoulder. (5) Lift your right forearm to strike your attacker under the jaw as your right foot blocks his right leg below his knee, as close to his ankle as possible. Your right knee should be bent slightly against his right leg. Before executing the throw be sure you are balanced. This is initially done by looking directly forward and down. (If you can see your left kneecap and, directly below it, the front of your left foot, you should be well balanced for the throw. As you develop a feel for the throw this will no longer be necessary.) (6) Straighten your right leg sharply as you pull with your left hand and push with your right, turning to your left (all at the same time). Be sure to keep your entire body in a straight line from your right foot to your shoulders. (7) Once your opponent is down slide your left hand so that your left thumb is on the back of his right hand and your fingers are underneath. (8) Bring your right thumb and fingers next to your left hand to grab his wrist as you drop down on his bicep (optional move) with your left kneecap for the submission. Dropping fast can break his wrist.

42

LEG LIFT/GROIN STOMP

(1) Your attacker grabs you from behind, pinning your arms with a bear-hug. (2) Bring your leg up and (3) stomp down on his instep with your heel, causing him to relax his grip. (4) Shift your right leg to the outside of his right leg as you bend over quickly to grab his right leg just above his ankle. (5) Lift his leg up to your right thigh, throwing him off balance. (6) Be sure that you stop his foot at the upper part of your right thigh, and not in the middle of your groin. (7) Stomp down with the heel of your left foot into your attacker's groin.

DROP THROW /
CHEEKBONE STRIKE

(1) Your attacker sets a rear forearm choke with his right arm and pulls you so that your back is slightly arched. Have your left leg forward. (2) Strike your attacker hard in his lower left ribs with your left elbow. Your right hand then reaches up and (3) grabs his right shoulder. Grab his right elbow (or sleeve) with your left hand. (4) Hold tight and drop straight down onto your right knee. Your right kneecap should be just in front of his right foot so that his right leg is blocked. (5) Turn to your left as you drop, causing your opponent to be thrown over your shoulder. (6) Keep hold of his right sleeve or wrist and (7) strike his right cheekbone with your right palm.

2

4

5

7

THROAT (TRACHEA) ATTACK

(1) You are attacked with a two-handed front choke. (2) Bring your right hand up and extend your fingertips until they rest on your attacker's trachea just below his larynx, (see inset 2A for detail.) (3) Keeping your fingers straight, thrust against the attacker's trachea and straighten your arm. (Inset 3A shows how your arm moves in comparison to your attacker's original position.) (4) Once your arm is fully extended keep it fully extended, stepping forward with your

right foot to execute the technique. To throw your opponent backward (as shown), direct the force of your fingers slightly upward, toward the back of his head. If you want him to go directly down, direct the force of your fingertips downward. In a life or death situation this technique could be used as a strike rather than a press. Striking the trachea and/or larynx at this point can cause the trachea to collapse or go into spasms, suffocating your opponent.

CHIN OR NOSE TURN / ELBOW STRIKE

(1) Your attacker sets a headlock with his right arm. (2) Bring your left hand up under your attacker's chin (or, as shown in 2A, your middle finger under his nose) and (3) turn his head to his left. (4) Be sure to turn your attacker's head to his left by *pushing*. Do *not* pull it back. (5) As he turns and releases his hold, slip your head out of the headlock. (6) Slide your left hand down and around so that your left forearm is under his chin, placing him in a headlock under your armpit. (7) Strike your opponent's back with your right elbow just inside of his left shoulderblade for a finishing blow. Be sure that your closed fist is facing you as you strike.

BASIC HAND THROW / WRIST OR ELBOW SNAP SUBMISSION

(1) Assume a ready position as you are threatened with a knife. (2) Pivot your right foot back thus moving your body out of the way of the straight knife thrust (note arrow indicating movement of right foot). Reach for the wrist of his knife hand from behind after his knife hand has passed your left hand. (3) Your left hand grabs the attacker's right hand on top of his wrist (so he can't bend his hand) with your thumb between his third and fourth knuckle on the back of his hand (see inset 3A). Both thumbs may also be put between his third and fourth knuckles, or you could also strike his knife hand with your right kneecap to dislodge the knife. (4) Step forward with your right foot as your right hand strikes the back of his right hand with your thumb still in place. (5) Pivot your left leg back (as indicated by arrow) in a counterclockwise direction as you push his bent hand with your right hand. (6) Turn his hand in a counterclockwise direction as you continue to pivot your left foot back until you (7) bring opponent down. (8) For a wrist or elbow snap submission place your right instep tight against his right armpit with your foot on the ground and his elbow just below your kneecap. Keep his wrist bent down (and his arm straight) and turn it to the left as you turn to your left. Have your left leg away from the attacker for balance. (9) If the attacker still has the knife, take it away from him before releasing him. For the submission (9A) place your left thumb next to your right thumb behind his hand. This hold can also be used for the throw.

OUTER SWEEPING HIP THROW

(1) Assume a ready position facing your attacker. (2) Block your attacker's right punch outward with your left forearm, leaning in slightly toward your attacker. (3) Block his left punch outward with your right forearm. Slide your left hand down and hook onto the attacker's right forearm with your fingers on top and thumb underneath. (4) Push the attacker's left arm away and down in a clockwise circle with your right forearm. Do not grab his left arm with your right hand at any time. (5) Move his left arm across his chest toward his right side as you step and pivot in for a basic hip throw. (6) Grab

attacker at his right shoulder with your right hand. This will trap his left arm across his chest and behind your body. (7) Squat down to set the throw (as for a basic hip throw). You should be set so that you can balance on your left foot when the throw is executed. (8) Sweep your right leg back, keeping it straight, and making contact on the lower part of the attacker's right shin (9) as you turn your body to the left (as in a hip throw) to sweep your opponent off of the ground. (10) From this position you can drop your right knee into the side of his chest or your left knee to his head.

7

9

10

CORKSCREW

(1) As you are threatened with a knife, assume a ready position. (2) Execute a crossblock, with your right forearm crossed over your left forearm and hands open (fingers together). Meet the force of the attack straight on, deflecting the direction of the blow to your right. Step forward as you block and keep your legs bent slightly so they can absorb the shock of the blow. (3) Grab the attacker's arm at his wrist with your right hand preventing him from moving his hand (and the knife). Your left hand also turns to grab his wrist. This can be done almost simultaneously as you start to bring the attacker's arm down (4) to your right in a clockwise circle, securing your grab with both hands. Your hands should be grabbing his wrist like a baseball bat (*note arrows*). (5) Continue winding his arm in the same direction as you step in under his arm until your right foot is even with the attacker's right foot. (6) Turn your body to your left by pivoting on the balls of your feet so you're facing in the same direction as the attacker. Continue to wind his arm, making a big circle. (7) Continue the wind and pull out and forward to execute the throw. Keep the knife pointed away from your body (if the attacker is still holding it). (8) With the throw completed, you may step forward with your right foot if necessary to maintain your balance. *Caution:* In practice, be sure to let your partner's wrist slide (don't hold it tight) as you wind his arm. As you're not really twisting his arm full force he should execute a forward roll for you out of courtesy so you can get the feel of the technique. Using full force on this technique can either cause immediate serious injury to the shoulder joint or subtle injury that is cumulative over the years.

ARMBAR (SHOULDERLOCK) REAR THROW / SHOULDERLOCK SUBMISSION

(1) Assume a ready position as you face an attacker. (2) If your attacker swings with an overhead club, cross-block in the same manner as the cork-screw technique. (3) Continue to block with your right forearm as your left hand grabs his right wrist and hand (the first two fingers of your left hand should be on the back of his right hand). (4) Release the block with your right forearm and use the outer edge of your right hand to strike down on the attacker's elbow to bend it. Bend his hand in at the same time by pushing with your left hand. (5) Move your right arm under his upper arm and clamp your right hand onto the back of his hand. Simultaneously step forward with your right foot. (6) Step forward with your left foot as you bring both of your hands straight down, forcing your attacker backward. In a street situation, remain standing as you bring your arms down. For safety's sake with your partner, execute this phase slowly and go only as fast as your partner can fall. It is quite possible to tear the shoulder out of its socket. (7) If you choose to do a shoulderlock submission, drop down with the attacker onto your right knee. Your left hand should rest on the back of his elbow. Push his elbow away from you as you pull his wrist toward you for the submission.

ARMBAR WINDING THROW /
ARMBAR SUBMISSION

(1) As your attacker grabs you with his left hand and pulls you toward him, lean in slightly (2) so you can more easily block his hit effectively with your left forearm. (3) Bring your right hand across and deliver a backhand strike (4) to the side or base of his ribs. You may also strike his cheekbone (see inset 4A). (5) Move your left hand over the attacker's right arm and then under it at, or slightly above, his elbow. Your right hand rests on his right shoulder. Clamp your left hand onto your right forearm, thumb and fingers on top. His right wrist is now trapped in your armpit, and his palm should be up with the outside of his elbow facing down. (6) Raise your left forearm slightly and push down with your right hand to create pain in your attacker's elbow locked in the armbar. (He will go up onto his toes.) (7) Keep pressure against the outside of his elbow with your left forearm as you pivot back on your left foot, throwing him. Exercise caution with your partner here. (8) Bring him down to the ground, keeping hold of the armbar position. (9) For a submission hold drop down onto your right knee, make sure the armbar is set tight, and lean up and back slightly for submission.

2

3

5

6

8

9

OUTER REAR SWEEPING THROW

(1) Assume a ready position facing your opponent. (2) Block his right punch outward and to your left with your left forearm. Step in slightly with your left foot to keep your balance. (3) Move your left foot to the outside of his right foot so that your left foot is parallel to or slightly behind his right foot, but pointed opposite from his direction. (4) Your right hand

reaches across and grabs your attacker's left lapel to help push him off balance as your right leg comes up to sweep his right leg from behind. (5) Sweep his leg up causing the attacker to fall backward. Be sure to lean forward to protect your own balance. (6) Drop your right knee onto the side of his ribs for a finishing blow.

NECK THROW / SCISSOR-CHOKE SUBMISSION

(1) Assume a ready position facing your opponent. (2) Block your attacker's punch outward with your left forearm as you step in with your left foot. (3) Slide your left hand down his arm and grab his sleeve while bringing your right hand up inside his left arm. (4) Strike the side of his neck sharply with your cupped right hand just below the ear (you should hear a "pop" when you hit) and step in with your right foot. The strike will shock the middle ear and cause your opponent a momentary loss of balance. (5) Pivot back on your left foot as you pull your attacker's right arm with your left hand and continue the motion of your right hand, turning to the left, (6) bringing your opponent down. (7) Set a forearm scissor-choke submission by gripping your right arm with your left hand (7A) from behind your opponent's neck while your right hand is pressed underneath his left ear. You may also press the nerves behind the trapezeus muscle (7B) along with the scissor-choke submission to create additional pain.

2

4

5

7A

7

7B

INNER SWEEPING HIP THROW / KNEE-DROP SUBMISSION

(1) Assume a ready position facing your attacker. (2) Block his right punch with your left forearm. (3) Step in close with your right foot, pivoting on your left foot. Your right arm should go underneath his left arm around his body. (This is just one method of grabbing your opponent for a hip throw. Other ways are shown throughout the text. Usually the height and weight of your opponent will determine how you grab him with your

right hand.) (4) Hold the attacker tight against you. Your right foot should be just inside and in front of his right foot. Your right hip does not block his right hip as much as in the basic hip throw. (5) Push your right foot and leg outward against his, to sweep his leg out and up. Continue to move as with a basic hip throw, balancing on your left leg. (6) Once your opponent is thrown, drop your right knee into his armpit for submission.

STOMACH THROW / LAPEL CHOKE

(1) When your attacker pushes you, (2) grab your attacker's right sleeve with your left hand and his left lapel with your right hand. (3) As you start to fall back, pulling him toward you, place your right foot in the center of his stomach. (4) Roll onto the ground. To execute the throw, push the attacker with your right foot. If you don't want to submit the attacker let go of his sleeve and lapel as his body passes your head. In practice, keep hold of

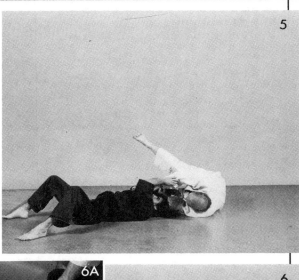

your partner. (5) For the submission keep hold of the attacker and roll over next to him by (6) rolling on your left knee to come up onto your right foot, as shown. Your right hand has brought his left lapel over to the right side of his neck, with your right thumb into the nerve of his neck. Pull up with your left hand, automatically setting the choke and nerve attack. (Inset 6A shows where your thumb should be pressing on his neck.)

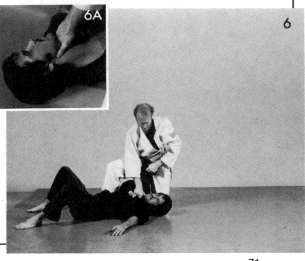

FLOATING DROP THROW / SHOULDERLOCK PIN

(1) Assume a ready position facing your attacker. (2) Block his right punch with your left forearm, then (3) step in with your left foot and grab his sleeve with your left hand. (4) Put your right arm around the attacker's head and kick your right leg to the outside of his right leg as high as it will go. Have your left leg follow your right leg so that you have both feet up in the air, your back tight against the attacker's chest and (for safety's sake) his head tight against you. (5) Turn quickly to your left as you reach your maximum height to bring your opponent over you and down. Make sure your partner gives a kiai on this throw. The remaining photographs show the shoulderlock pin from the opposite side. (6-8) To set a shoulderlock pin, bring your right leg over the lower part of the attacker's right arm, bending his arm back (his elbow can be broken at this point if he can't bend his elbow by hooking your right foot under your left knee joint and straightening your left leg). Maintain the headlock. (9) Once his arm is bent, with his palm up, bring your right leg down, turning toward your attacker's head and bringing your left leg up as shown. (10) Continue this motion, bringing your shin back to your body as you lean forward against his elbow.

FORWARD FINGER THROW

(1) Your attacker has grabbed your left wrist. Keep your left hand relaxed and open at all times. (This makes it much more difficult for the attacker to sense what you're doing until it's too late for him to do anything about it.) Start to turn *only* your hand, (not your whole arm, and do *not* lift your arm) in a counterclockwise motion (2) over his hand and to your left. Your arm should follow your hand. As your attacker starts to lose his grip grab his fingers (2A) with your right hand. (3) Turn to your left on the balls of your feet and bend his fingers back until he's on

his toes. Then push his fingers forward by keeping your wrist locked and applying pressure to the backs of his fingers just below his knuckles. Push outward and slightly upward to execute the throw. (4) Complete the circle by bringing your hand out, down, and back. (5) For a submission drop down onto your right knee, press his palm to the ground and bend his fingers back. *Note:* In practice, grab at least three fingers for this technique. It will give you greater control and reduce the chance of accidentally breaking your partner's fingers.

BODY WINDING THROW / ARMBAR TO SHOULDERLOCK PIN

(1) Assume a ready position facing your attacker. When your attacker starts a sideswipe swing to your head, (2) lean forward to block with your left forearm, stepping forward with your left foot if necessary, to get your head out of line of his club swing. (3) Your left hand grabs the attacker's sleeve or arm. Turn in (*as shown by the arrow*) so that you are tight against his body. Thrust your right arm over his right arm, shoving his right shoulder under your right armpit. (4) Block his right leg with your right leg. Lean forward, keeping your entire body straight, turning to your left as you fall. Your right hand may grab onto the attacker's right arm, but it should be done loosely to avoid the chance of injuring your right elbow. (5) When you both hit the ground, be sure your partner kiais! (6) Once you're on the ground your right arm goes underneath the attacker's right arm and clamps (palm down with your thumb and fingers on top) onto your left forearm. Your right forearm should be just above his elbow. His arm should be palm up. (7) Push down with your left forearm (just above your wrist) on his right arm (just above his wrist) to cause your attacker to release the weapon. *Note:* In practice, if his arm bends or the outside of his elbow is not facing down, help him bend his arm while keeping hold as shown. Your left hand should then bring his arm down with the back of his hand on the ground, his wrist bent, and his palm up. (8) Lean forward, pulling slightly with your left hand, as you turn to your left to execute the shoulderlock. Keep your body against his.

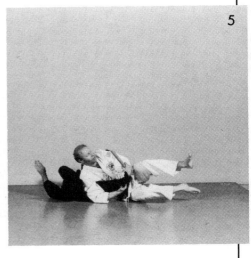

LEG LIFT THROW

(1) Assume a ready position facing your attacker. (2) As your attacker throws a front snap kick, sidestep to your left with your left foot. At the same time your right arm blocks outward to deflect the leg and hook it from underneath. (3) After catching your attack-

3

er's calf in the crook of your elbow, step forward with your right leg and reach for the attacker's face with your right hand to execute the throw. (4) Follow through completely by stepping forward with your left leg if necessary to retain your balance.

4

INNER REAR SWEEPING THROW / GROIN ATTACK

(1) Assume a ready position facing your attacker. (2) As your attacker throws a front snap kick, sidestep to your right while leaning to your right to get out of the direct line of his kick. (3) Deflect the blow with your left forearm as you slip your arm under his right leg. (4) Step forward with your left foot and grab the attacker's left shoulder with your right hand. (5) Bring your right leg behind your attacker's left leg and sweep his leg up (6) as you lean forward. Keep your right leg straight as you sweep. (7) Take your right hand off of the attacker's right lapel and either: (7A) strike to his groin with your fist, (7B) pull his testicles with your right hand, or (7C) drop your right knee into his groin.

KNUCKLE-PRESS TAKEDOWN

(1) Assume a ready position facing your attacker. (2) Your attacker grabs your hair with his right hand. (3) Bring both of your hands up and grab his hand, with his knuckles in the middle of your palms, and your fingers interlocked, trapping his hand on

your head. (4) Deliver a front kick with either leg into his groin. (5) Lift his hand off of your head, keeping his knuckles squeezed together. (6) Bend his hand back as you push his arm down to bring the attacker down. Keep your body straight.

WRISTLOCK-LIFT COME-ALONG / ARMLOCK COME-ALONG

(1) When your attacker grabs your hair from behind, (2) grab the attacker's hand with both of your hands. (Your thumbs are under his wrist and your fingers are over his knuckles.) Hold his hand to your head. (3) Pivot your left foot back and turn into the attacker until you're facing him, keeping his hand trapped against your head. (4) Remove his hand from your head, keeping his wrist twisted and his hand in line with the rest of his arm. (5) Bring the attacker onto his toes by exerting upward pressure at his knuckles. As long as upward pressure can be maintained your attacker can be controlled. (6) Step around to the back of your attacker and (7) bring his arm behind him, lifting up. (8) As you bring his arm up bend his wrist, slide your left hand away and slide your right hand onto the back of his hand with your fingers pointing up and his fingers pointing out. His knuckles should be in the palm of your hand. (9) To set the come-along make sure that his right elbow is trapped against you. Pull your right hand toward you to exert pressure, create pain, and control the attacker. *Note:* This is a *proper hold*. Resistance to any proper hold causes serious pain and can quite easily result in a fractured joint.

NERVE WHEEL THROW

(1) Assume a ready position facing your attacker. (2) As your attacker attempts a bear hug, grab his flesh at the side or base of his ribs (each side), thus attacking nerves (inset 2A) and causing your attacker to release his hold. (Continue turning your hands inward toward his body to cause additional pain. Not only are you digging in deeper with your fingers this way, but the increased pressure of your fingers is also increasing your con-

3

4

trol.) Step forward with your right foot toward your attacker. (3&4) Pivot your left foot back and turn your hands to your left, as if you're turning a steering wheel to your left. The pain you are creating should cause him to leave the ground—to get away from the pain. (5) Once your attacker is on the ground, you can go to a submission. If you try to lift the attacker to do the throw you're doing it incorrectly.

5

THUMB WINDING THROW

(1) Your attacker approaches from behind, preparing to choke you. (2) Reach over your shoulder to grab the attacker's thumbs. Grab his thumbs securely (see inset 2A) with your hands, thumbs down. (Grabbing his little fingers is a good second choice.) (3) Lift his hands off and turn to your right. (Inset 3A shows how the attacker's thumbs are held at this stage.) (4) Bring his left arm down across his right arm, at his elbows, thus causing his left elbow to be locked against his right arm. (5) Wind both of his thumbs in a large counterclockwise circle, keeping them at opposite poles on the "edge" of the circle, to execute the throw. Let go of his thumbs once the attacker is thrown.

2

2A

4

5

SLEEVE PIVOT THROW

(1) Assume a ready position facing your attacker. (2) Your attacker grabs your right wrist and pulls you toward him. Do not resist his pull. You're going to use his strength. (3) Step with your right foot behind attacker, in the direction of his pull, using his pulling force to give you momentum. (4) Grab his right sleeve or arm as you pivot to your left. (5) Pivot your left foot back, going down on your left knee, and con-

4

5

tinue pulling his sleeve. (6) When your opponent falls, do not attempt to release your right hand while this technique is being executed. Your hand can be easily turned out once the throw is completed. This throw can be done quite fast and easily if the attacker keeps hold of your right wrist. The throw can still be done if your attacker lets go as long as you've made it to step 4.

6

WRISTLOCK TAKEDOWN

(1) Assume a ready position facing your attacker, who has a knife in his belt. (2) Aś he draws his knife for a forward thrust prepare to crossblock. (Your,right arm crosses over your left arm midway down both forearms. Your hands are open but your fingers are together.) Step forward slightly and flex your legs to absorb the shock. (3) Block hard. This will cause your attacker to drop his knife if done correctly. (4) Your left hand continues to block while your right hand reaches over your left and grabs his knife hand with your thumb between his first and second knuckles and your fingers under his wrist. Bend his wrist by pushing with your thumb. Start to turn it in a large clockwise circle. (5) As his hand comes up in a clockwise circle discontinue the block with your left forearm so that your left hand holds the attacker's hand with your thumbs next to each other. (6) Push the knuckles of his hand away from you by pushing with your thumbs while keeping his arm straight by pulling at the base of his hand with your fingers. This small circular motion will cause your opponent to go down. If he moves toward you, take a step away from him and continue the pressure. (7) If he resists the takedown, or if you think he might, a good swift kick to the chest or solar plexus will loosen him up. (8) Drop down onto your right knee as he goes down. Keep your back straight. (9) Press his hand toward his body using your thumbs for a submission.

SHOULDERLOCK REAR TAKEDOWN

(1) Your attacker shakes your right hand (what may be perceived as a friendly gesture might actually be a way of preventing you from using your right hand to defend yourself). (2) Slap your left hand onto the back of his right hand and grip firmly with your thumb over the top of his wrist and your fingers underneath. (3) Step in with your left foot and bring his hand up in a counterclockwise circle to your right. (4) As you continue to turn his arm counterclockwise bring it over your head, pivoting your body to your right.

Your right hand maintains the handshake. (5) Continue turning until you are facing in the opposite direction from your attacker. You should be as close to the attacker as possible during steps 4 and 5 to prevent him from turning out of the technique. His shoulder is now locked. (6) Pull straight down with your left and right hands to take the attacker down. In practice, pull down only as fast as your partner can go down and drop onto your right knee.

SHOULDERLOCK COME-ALONG

(1) Your attacker shakes your right hand (what may be perceived as a friendly gesture might actually be a way of preventing you from using your right hand to defend yourself). (2) Slap your left hand onto the back of his right hand and grip firmly with your thumb over the top of his wrist and your fingers underneath. (3) Step in with your left foot and bring his hand up in a counterclockwise circle to your right. (4) As you continue to turn his arm counterclockwise bring it over your head, pivoting your body to your right. Your right hand maintains the handshake. (5) Continue turning until you are facing in the opposite direction from your attacker. You should be as close to the attacker as possible during steps 4 and 5 to prevent him from turning out of the technique. His shoulder is now locked. (6) Your right hand keeps hold of the handshake. Your left hand lets go of his wrist and grabs his elbow (7&8) as you turn around so you're facing the same direction as the attacker. Pull his elbow to you thus arching his back. Keep the handshake next to his back. Your left forearm should be resting against the rear base of his skull to provide support for the hold. You can walk attacker anywhere you want with this hold. Pain is controlled by pulling his arm by his elbow with your left hand.

ELBOW-TURN TAKEDOWN

(1) Assume a ready position facing your attacker. (2) When your attacker grabs your clothing with both hands, (3) bring your right hand (palm up and slightly cupped) up to your attacker's left elbow. Bring your left hand (palm down) over his right forearm and under his left forearm as close to you as possible. (4) Use your right hand to push his elbow and turn it to your left in a counterclockwise circle as the back of your left hand comes up against the inside of his left forearm. Turn to your left as you raise his elbow. (Inset 4A shows how your fingers point in the direction of the circle.) (5) Continue pivoting. Your left hand turns away from you and grabs the attacker's left forearm (thumb underneath and fingers on top) (6) Continue to roll his elbow, bringing the attacker down. (7) If brought down swiftly the shoulder will strike the ground first, causing severe injury, due to the momentum created by rolling his elbow.

ARMBAR WINDING THROW / NECK-SCISSOR SUBMISSION

(1) Your attacker grabs your right shoulder from behind with his right hand. (2) Pivot your left foot back and turn to face the attacker. As you turn, bring your left arm up in a counter-clockwise circle to your left to protect you in case the attacker attempts a strike with his left hand as you turn. (3&4) Your left arm goes over his right arm and comes up underneath his elbow as your right hand

3

4

rests on the attacker's right shoulder. (5) Clamp onto your right forearm with your left hand, thumb and fingers on top. His right wrist should be in your armpit, his palm up and the outside of his elbow facing down. Raise your left forearm up slightly and push down slightly with your right hand to create pain in the attacker's elbow, which should be locked in the

5

Continued on next page

armbar. (6) Keep pressure against his elbow with your left forearm as you pivot your left foot back, throwing your opponent. (7) Bring him down to the ground. Drop onto your right knee. (8) Set armbar and neck scissor by pulling the attacker up slightly and bringing your left leg around in front of his neck. (9) Lean back, sliding your right foot under the back of his head. If you hold the

armbar firmly it will cause his neck to move higher up between your legs. (10) Scissor his neck by interlocking your feet and straightening your legs. (Don't squeeze your legs to choke your opponent. Your leg muscles aren't designed for squeezing. They operate more effectively if you straighten them.) Lean back to execute armbar submission at the same time.

HAND-WIND / ELBOW-ROLL TAKEDOWN

(1) Your attacker has his right hand over your mouth and his left hand holding your left arm back. (2) Loosen up the attacker and distract him by either scraping your right heel down his shin and/or (3) stomping down on his right instep with your right heel. (You may even bite or spit on his hand.) (4) Keeping your left hand open and relaxed, turn your hand up counterclockwise (left) as you pivot to your left. As you bring his arm up your left thumb should go under his arm so you can grab his wrist. A secure hold is desired, but a tight grip is not essential. (5) Bring your right hand, slightly cupped, up under his elbow and roll (push) it in the same counterclockwise direction. (6) Continue to pivot counterclockwise and push against his elbow. (7) Bring your attacker to the ground. (8) Rest your right kneecap on his upper arm (half way between his shoulder and elbow) for the submission.

HAND-WIND /
ELBOW-ROLL TAKEDOWN

(1) Your attaker's right hand grips your right wrist in an armlock behind your back. (2) Make a fist with your right hand and use your left hand to grab your right fist. (See inset 2A for detail). (3) Holding your arm in place in relation to your body, squat down slightly as your left foot sidesteps to your left. Your left hand then pushes down on your right fist as your body moves to the left. Your right foot does not move to the left. This move will put your right arm and hand at your right side rather than behind you and the attacker's hold can be broken. (4) Let go with your left hand and open up your right hand. Turn your right hand in a clockwise circle to your right as you turn to face your opponent. Your right thumb should be under his wrist so you can grab his wrist. (5) Turn to face your attacker by bringing your left foot around. Cup your left hand and push it up under his elbow. (6) Raise his elbow up in a clockwise direction while turning to your right. Note that the left hand is *not* grabbing his elbow. If the palm is kept cupped it can act as a socket, rotating so that your fingers can point in the direction you wish him to go (this is using ki). (7) Continue to pivot and push your opponent's elbow to bring him down. (8) Drop down on your left knee. Executing a takedown quickly can result in serious shoulder injury to your partner.

ELBOW LIFT

(1) Your attacker approaches from behind and (2) grabs your right sleeve with his left hand. (3) Turn to your right toward your attacker, raising your right arm and turning it in a clockwise circle to your right. (4) By stepping toward him, your attacker's arm will bend slightly with your forearm up against the outside of his elbow. (5) Continue the circular movement (keep your palm facing down), raising his elbow up to get him off balance. (5A) To set a come-along hold, clamp onto your left forearm with your right hand and raise your right forearm just enough to keep your attacker up on his toes. (6) The upward force of this move causes the attacker to fall backward. (7) Follow through even after the attacker has let go and fallen.

2

5A

5

4

7

HEAD WINDING THROW

(1) Your attacker grabs your clothing. (2) Strike your attacker's solar plexus with your right fist to loosen him up, putting your right shoulder into the punch to maximize the force of the strike. (3) Bring your left hand up around the side of his head and grab his hair on the opposite side (the left side). To grab the hair properly your fingers should be spread apart. Slide your hand up around the attacker's head, starting from the base of his head, until your hand is where you want it. Close your hand, grabbing as much hair as close to the skull as possible. This is more painful and gives *much better* control (as compared to a loose grab of a few hairs) and actually reduces the chance of hair being pulled out because of the larger area affected. (4) Cup your right hand at the base of the attacker's chin. Pull his hair toward you from the left and push chin away in a counterclockwise motion to your left. (5) You may need to bring your right foot forward slightly for balance. (6) Pivot your left foot back and continue turning the attacker's head counterclockwise. Turn it—don't pull it. (7) Bring your opponent down. Drop to your right knee and (8) quickly turn your opponent's head the other way to snap the neck. (Life or death situation only!)

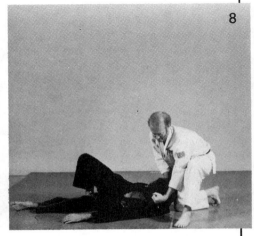

REAR LEG-LIFT THROW

(1) Your attacker has you in a head-lock, using his right arm. (2) With your left hand, grab the back of your attacker's collar (or his hair). Your right palm rests behind his right knee joint, thumb down. (3) Press the nerve just inside his gastrocnemius muscle (see inset 3A) behind the knee joint. This will cause his leg to jerk up automatically. If this doesn't work try pinching the inside of the attacker's thigh very quickly just above the knee joint with the nails of your right thumb and index finger. (4) As he lifts his leg continue to raise it further. At the same time pivot your left leg back and out of the way as you yank down on his collar. (5) Follow your attacker down to the ground (in case he keeps hold with the headlock), dropping onto your left knee. (6&7) Grab his groin with your right hand and pull.

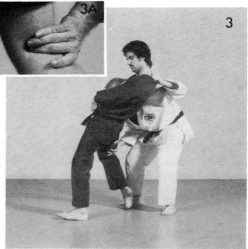

2

4

5

7

1

2

LAPEL WHEEL THROW

(1) Your attacker grabs your clothing with both hands. (2) Bring your left hand up and grab the attacker's left lapel as high as possible, your palm facing out. Then grab his opposite lapel at about mid-chest height with your right hand. (3) Pull your attacker toward you with your right hand to set the choke. (It is not necessary to push with your left hand to set the choke. Let your right hand do all the work.)

3

(4) Step back with your left foot as you pivot to your left to throw. Your right hand should continue pulling his right lapel and your left forearm should be firmly lodged under his chin, choking him. (5) Go down onto your left knee to finish throw. (6) Pull up on his right lapel with your right hand to choke. Your left knee should be against the back of his head for support.

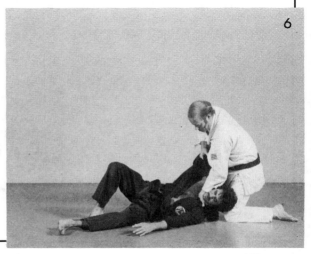

HIP THROW /
WRISTLOCK-LIFT SUBMISSION

(1) Your attacker attempts a knife swipe. (2) Lean back slightly and side-step to your left to get out of the path of his knife. (3) Once the knife has passed move back in and make a fist with both hands, (4) stepping in with your right foot and bring both fore-arms up to block his back swing. (5) Block hard. (Fists are needed here due to his much greater force with a back swing.) Your left forearm should block above the attacker's elbow while your right forearm blocks his lower fore-arm. (6) Before your opponent recov-ers from the blow, bend the attacker's arm by pushing with your right fore-arm. Do not grab his forearm with your right hand as he will be able to resist if you do. Open your right hand as you

116

Continued on next page

bend his arm back. (7) Bring your left forearm over his upper arm and clamp onto your right forearm. (The hold is shown more clearly in step 9). At this point you may execute a rear shoulderlock takedown (not shown) by pushing down with your right forearm and stepping forward with your right leg, then going down onto your right knee, as on page 61. (8) To execute a hip throw swing your body around, bringing your left foot back against your opponent with your right hip blocking his. Hold the shoulderlock tight against you. (9) Execute the throw, going down onto your right knee. (10) To set a wristlock lift, slide your right hand down to the back of his hand so his knuckles are resting in the palm of your hand. (11) Lift up at the knuckles to break his wrist, (12) or to raise your opponent up so you can set a neck scissor along with the wristlock. (13) Lean back to set the scissors.

8

9

12

13

This chart shows specific techniques in this book that can be applied to a variety of attacks. While there would be no modification in the actual execution of the specific technique, it would be necessary to modify your initial response (for example, block, release, strike, etc.) to the specific attack from what was shown in the text.

	single lapel	double lapel	front choke	rear choke	rear forearm choke	headlock	rear shoulder grab
Basic One-Arm Hip Throw	✓	✓	✓	✓	✓	✓	✓
Basic Drop Throw	✓	✓	✓	✓	✓	✓	✓
Leg Lift					✓		
Drop Throw	✓	✓	✓	✓	✓		
Throat (Trachea) Attack	✓	✓	✓				
Chin or Nose Turn						✓	
Hand Throw	✓	✓	✓			✓	
Outside Sweeping Hip Throw	✓	✓	✓	✓	✓	✓	✓
Corkscrew						✓	
Armbar Rear Throw							
Armbar Winding Throw	✓	✓					
Outer Rear Sweeping Throw	✓						
Neck Throw	✓	✓	✓				✓
Inner Sweeping Hip Throw	✓	✓	✓		✓		✓
Stomach Throw	✓	✓	✓				
Floating Drop Throw							
Forward Finger Throw						✓	
Body Winding Throw	✓	✓					✓
Leg Lift Throw							
Inner Rear Sweeping Throw	✓	✓					
Knuckle-Press Takedown	✓						
Wristlock-Lift							
Wheel Throw	✓	✓	✓				
Thumb Winding Throw				✓			
Sleeve Pivot Throw							
Wristlock Takedown	✓	✓				✓	
Shoulderlock Rear Takedown							
Shoulderlock Come-Along							
Elbow-Turn Takedown	✓	✓	✓				
Elbow-Roll Takedown							
Elbow Lift							
Head Winding Throw	✓	✓	✓	✓			
Lapel Wheel Throw	✓	✓	✓				
Hip Throw							

DIFFERENT

BASIC JUJITSU TECHNIQUES

TYPES OF ATTACKS

rear bearhug	front bearhug	single hit	double hit	overhead club	sideswipe club	overhead knife	straight knife	knife swipe	handshake	wrist grab	kick	push	grab & hit	hair grab	mugging	arm grab
✓	✓	✓	✓	✓	✓	✓			✓	✓		✓	✓		✓	
✓	✓	✓	✓	✓	✓				✓	✓	✓	✓	✓		✓	
✓															✓	
✓	✓	✓													✓	
	✓	✓	✓	✓					✓	✓	✓		✓			
	✓	✓	✓	✓	✓	✓	✓	✓		✓						
✓	✓	✓	✓	✓		✓				✓		✓	✓		✓	
	✓	✓	✓	✓		✓			✓	✓						
				✓		✓										
	✓	✓	✓	✓									✓			
	✓	✓	✓	✓									✓			
	✓	✓	✓	✓	✓					✓			✓			
✓	✓	✓	✓	✓						✓			✓			
	✓	✓								✓		✓	✓			
	✓		✓													
✓	✓	✓							✓	✓			✓			
✓	✓	✓	✓	✓				✓								
											✓					
	✓	✓	✓								✓					
														✓		
														✓		
	✓												✓			
	✓	✓		✓						✓						
✓	✓		✓		✓					✓			✓			
							✓									
							✓									
	✓	✓														
															✓	
																✓
✓	✓	✓											✓			
					✓			✓								
	✓				✓			✓								

121

APPENDIX

SCORING CRITERIA FOR RANK (BELT) EXAMINATIONS

Listed below are the standards used by the AJA for scoring the various belt examinations. Keep in mind that this is a guide. The person who is testing you may score in between any of the scores below.

A person taking the green belt examination must average 4.3 on the performance part, assuming they earn a full 28 points on their attitude (ki). A score of five or higher is extremely rare on the green belt examination.

A person taking the purple belt examination must average 4.63 on the performance part, assuming they earn a full 28 points on their attitude. A score higher than five is still rare although there might be a few exceptions.

A person taking any of the brown belt examinations must average 5.25 on the performance part of the test. Your attitude is a major factor in deciding whether you are worthy of the rank you are being considered for.

Score	Criteria
(0)	Unable to execute a technique or wrong technique executed.
(1) Poor	Must be told or shown how technique is done. Barely able to execute technique. Severe loss of balance.
(2) Very Awkward	Very awkward execution of technique. Poor balance. Verbal assistance required. Technique or moves must be repeated at least once.
(3) Barely Effective, Awkward	Somewhat awkward. Poor balance. Some verbal assistance required. Probably repeats or has to repeat moves or technique.
(4) Effective	Technique done fairly smoothly. Little hesitancy in movements. Good balance. No verbal assistance required. No repetition of moves or technique.
(5) Good	Technique done very smoothly. Well balanced. No hesitancy displayed at any time. Return to *tachi waza*. Kiai and/or appropriate submission.
(6) Very Good	Exceptionally good form. Very fluid movement. Execution appears effortless. Kiai and return to *tachi waza*. Submission suitable to technique.
(7) Excellent	Excellent form and execution. Jujitsu as an art.

On the following pages are sample score sheets for the green, purple and brown belt examinations, based on AJA standards.

Student's Name_____Number_____Date_____

GREEN BELT PROMOTIONAL EXAMINATION

A student may be able to pass this examination after about 18-36 hours of instruction plus additional time working on the techniques.

The student will be required to demonstrate 12 forms, techniques or variations, all of which must be different.

Scoring will be computed as follows:
(0) Unable to execute   (3) Barely effective
(1) Poor   (4) Effective
(2) Very awkward   (5) Good

93 points (70%) are required to pass.

PASSED: Yes_____
         No_____

_____
Instructor's Signature

UKEMI—BREAK FALLS
Mae Ukemi (forward roll/fall) ...... _____
Yoko Ukemi (side fall) .... _____
Ushiro Ukemi (backward roll/fall)... _____

     TOTAL UKEMI .... _____

KATA—FORMS
Koshi Nage (basic hip throw) ...... _____
Tai-Otoshi (basic drop throw) ...... _____
Te No Tatake (blocking hits)....... _____
Juji (crossblocks) .... _____
Shioku Waza (nerve technique) .... _____
Te Tatake (striking technique) ..... _____
Te Nage (basic hand throw) .... _____

     TOTAL KATA .... _____

WAZA—TECHNIQUES
For a hit .... _____
For a hit .... _____
For a shirt grab .... _____
For a front choke .... _____
For a bodygrab or headlock .... _____

     TOTAL WAZA .... _____

TOTAL UKEMI .... _____
TOTAL KATA .... _____
TOTAL WAZA.................. _____
ATTITUDE (KI) up to 28 points ..... _____

TOTAL EXAM .... _____

Student's Name_____Number_____Date_____

PURPLE BELT PROMOTIONAL EXAMINATION

A student may be able to pass this exam after 6-12 months or 50-75 additional hours of instruction after active involvement in the program as a green belt.

In order to pass the test the student will be expected to demonstrate 42 different forms, techniques, or variations (including eight submissions or come-alongs) and score a minimum of 191 points (70%) to pass.

The test is divided into two parts. You must score at least 74 points on Part 1 in order to go on to Part 2.

Scoring will be computed as follows using the *Scoring Criteria for Rank (Belt)*.

(7) Excellent, an art   (4) Effective, but awkward   (1) Poor
(6) Very good, fluid   (3) Barely effective, awkward   (0) Unable to execute
(5) Good, very smooth   (2) Very awkward

Part 1: KATA (FORMS) including 4-8 submits or come-alongs

Ippon Seoi Nage (one-arm hip throw) . . . ._____
Harai Goshi (outer sweeping hip throw)
or
Hane Goshi (inner sweeping hip throw) . .._____
Tomoenage (stomach throw) . . . . ._____
Uki-Otoshi (floating drop throw) . . . . . . ._____
Yubi Nage (finger throw). . . . . ._____
Karada Makikomi (body winding throw) . .._____
Ude Kudema (corkscrew) . . . . ._____
Ude Gurama Ushiro (armbar rear throw) . .._____
Ude Gurama Makikomi (armbar winding
   throw) . . . . ._____
Osoto Gari (outer rear sweeping throw) . .._____
Tai-Otoshi (body drop throw) . . . . ._____
Kubi Nage (neck throw). . . . . ._____
Kime-No-Kata (your choice of four additional forms or variations) . . . . ._____
_____
_____
_____

TOTAL KATA . . . . ._____

COMMENTS: _____
_____
_____
_____

Part 2: WAZA (TECHNIQUES) including 4-8 submits or come-alongs

Demonstrate a technique for:

Double hit. . . . . ._____
Lapel (shirt) grab and hit. . . . . ._____
Single or double wrist grab or handshake
   (do two of three). . . . . ._____
Rear or front choke, (close or far) or rear
   forearm choke ._____
Bearhug or waistgrab, front or rear . . . . . ._____
Kicks (two defenses). . . . . ._____
Knife attacks (two different). . . . . ._____
Rear shoulder or neck grab . . . . ._____
Hair grab (front, side, or back, one or two
   hands), or clothing grab (front, side, or
   back, one or two hands) . . . . ._____
Club attack. . . . . ._____
Freestyle (your choice of six more attacks, in addition to those listed above, which may be attacks your tester did *not* choose from the above list) . . . . . . ._____
_____
_____
_____
_____

TOTAL WAZA. . . . . ._____

COMPUTATION OF SCORES: Part 1 (KATA) . . . . ._____
Part 2 (WAZA). . . . . ._____
Attitude—Ki (up to 28 points). . . . . ._____

TOTAL SCORE . . . . ._____

Student's Name_____Number_____Date_____

BROWN BELT PROMOTIONAL EXAMINATION

A student may be able to pass the examination after a minimum of 50-100 hours (6-12 months) active participation in the program as a purple belt.

You must demonstrate ten forms and 15 defenses from the list below, selected at the time of the test. Your reaction to the attacks must be IMMEDIATE. You will be expected to know the names of the forms in Japanese and execute them without delay.

Scoring is as follows: (7) excellent; (6) very good; (5) good; (4) effective; (3) barely effective; (2) very awkward; (1) poor; (0) unable to execute. You must score 131 points (75%) in order to pass this portion of the examination.

KATA (FORMS) (10 selected)

Koshi Nage . . . . ._____
Tai Otoshi . . . . ._____
Ura Nage . . . . ._____
Ouchi Gari . . . . ._____
Shioku Waza . . . . ._____
Te Tatake . . . . ._____
Te Nage ._____
Ippon Seoi Nage . . . . ._____
Harai Goshi . . . . ._____
Hane Goshi . . . . ._____
Tomoenage . . . . ._____
Uki-Otoshi . . . . ._____
Yubi Nage . . . . ._____
Makikomi ._____
Ude Kudema . . . . ._____
Ude Gurama Makikomi . . . . ._____
Ude Gurama Ushiro . . . . ._____
Osoto Gari . . . . ._____
Kubi Nage . . . . ._____
Te Waza ._____
Ashi Waza . . . . ._____
Hiji Waza ._____
Shimi Waza . . . . ._____
Hiki Waza . . . . ._____
Tekubi Shimi Waza . . . . ._____

TOTAL KATA . . . . ._____
TOTAL WAZA . . . . ._____

TOTAL SCORE . . . . ._____

WAZA (TECHNIQUES) (15 selected)

Single Hit (left or right, high or low) . . . . ._____
Mugging Attack . . . . ._____
Club Attack (various) . . . . ._____
Kicks . . . . ._____
Handholds (single, double, front and rear) . . . . . . ._____
Armlock . . . . ._____
Headlock . . . . ._____
Reversing a Throw . . . . ._____
Being Pulled (forward, backward, sideways) . . . . ._____
Football Tackle . . . . ._____
Double Hits . . . . ._____
Hair Grabs (various) . . . . ._____
Knife Attacks (various) . . . . ._____
Lapel Grabs (single or double) . . . . ._____
Combination holds and attacks . . . . ._____
Cross Choke . . . . ._____
Multiple Attackers (usually two) . . . . ._____
Bearhugs and Waistgrabs (arm free or pinned,
    high or low) . . . . ._____
Nelsons (front and rear) . . . . ._____
Knife Threat . . . . ._____
Chokes (various) . . . . ._____
Handshakes . . . . ._____
Baton Attacks . . . . ._____
Reversing Opponent on Mat . . . . ._____
Shoulder Grabs (front and rear) . . . . ._____
Misc. Clothing Grabs . . . . ._____
Ground Defenses . . . . ._____

COMMENTS: _____
_____
_____

In addition to securing a passing score you must also have demonstrated a positive attitude toward the art and the class. If you are being examined for Ikkyu your examiner will also consider your potential as an instructor. Your examiner will be looking to see if you are developing a coherent style, suited to your physical stature, condition and agility.

If you pass the brown belt exam and the instructor feels that you are qualified to receive a brown belt, a Certificate of Promotion will be issued.

GLOSSARY

Come-along: A hold or lock on a person, usually applying pressure to a joint, that forces the person to move in a direction you desire; used in conjuction with a standing submission.

Deflect: Differs from a block in that you move the attacking limb out of the way, usually to your left or right, without stopping or significantly reducing the momentum of the attack.

Karate chop: A misnomer; actually a *shuto* or knife-edge strike using the outside part of the hand. Fingers are straight and together.

Kata: A specific form; such as a hip throw, nerve attack, submission, etc.

Loosen up: The use of one or a series of hits, nerve attacks, kicks, etc., to force your attacker's attention away from what you want to do, or to lessen his resistance to your defense.

Pinch: Also, "shark bite." A very slight pinch done with the tip of the thumb and index finger using the nails of both fingers, applied quickly to such areas as the inside of the upper arm, thighs, or sides of the rib cage; this creates a great deal of pain even if a person is resistant to nerve techniques.

Pivot: To move the designated foot backward (usually) in a large circle, left foot counterclockwise and right foot clockwise.

Ready Position: Your starting position for all defensive techniques in this book; allows you to face your opponent in a balanced stance with a minimum of your body exposed to attack. The feet should be approximately shoulder width apart and should always face the direction of the attacker if possible. May either be in a left or right ready position; your hands may either be clasped at your waist (left over right with your right in a gingitzu) if you do not wish to appear threatening, or with your left arm in a blocking position and right hand in a gingitzu for a more formal stance.

Standing submission: Finishing a technique with your opponent still standing, locked or held in a position where resistance by him or a continuation of the technique by you would result in injury to the attacker; usually involves pressure on or the locking of a bone joint (used in conjunction with a come-along).

Takedown: A technique, hold, lock, etc., designed to bring the attacker down without throwing him; the lock, hold, etc., is maintained throughout the technique and after the attacker is down.

Throw: A technique or hold designed to unbalance an attacker and physically lift him off the ground until he is down.

Waza: A combination of moves beginning with (1) a response to the attack, continuing with a (2) followthrough, and usually ending with a hold or strike that can be considered a (3) submission.

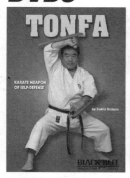
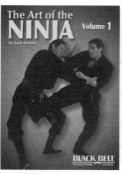

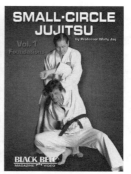